THE

ODDS

CHASE TWICHELL

THE ODDS

UNIVERSITY OF PITTSBURGH PRESS

Published by the University of Pittsburgh Press, Pittsburgh, Pa. 15260

Feffer and Simons, Inc., London
Manufactured in the United States of America

Library of Congress Cataloging in Publication Data

Twichell, Chase, 1950–
The odds.

(Pitt poetry series)
I. Title. II. Series.
PS3570.W4703 1986 811'.54 85-22562
ISBN 0-8229-3528-7
ISBN 0-8229-5377-3 (pbk.)

I'd like to thank the Bread Loaf Writers' Conference and the Artists Foundation in Boston for their support.

Thanks also to the editors of the following magazines, where poems were first published, sometimes in earlier forms: *Antaeus* ("A Fire in the Mind"); *Black Warrior Review* ("The Colorless Center of Everything" and "The Hotel du Nord"); "A Suckling Pig" and "Wine" originally appeared in *The Chowder Review*; *Crazyhorse* ("Cedar Needles" and "The Late Comers"); *Field* ("Not Like Water"); *Ironwood* ("Japanese Weeping Cherry"); *The Massachusetts Review* ("Paper White Narcissus"); *The Ohio Review* ("Evening, Herron's Farm"); *Parnassus: Poetry in Review* ("Religious Water"); *The Pennsylvania Review* ("Words for Synthesizer"); *Poetry* ("Abandoned House in Late Light" and "Blurry Cow"); *The Reaper* ("Cold, Substantial Clouds," "My Ruby of Lasting Sadness," and "Transfixed by the Swimmers"); *Sonora Review* ("In Bed with Books"); *Telescope* ("Asleep in the Heat," "Electrical Storm," and "Partita for Solo Violin"); *Tendril* ("Let X," "Meteor Showers, August, 1968," "The Moon in the Pines," "The Odds," and "Translations from the Rational"); and *The Threepenny Review* ("Rhymes for Old Age").

"Abandoned House in Late Light," "Blurry Cow," and "Paper White Narcissus" were reprinted in the *Anthology of Magazine Verse and Yearbook of American Poetry*, Monitor Book Company, Inc., Los Angeles, 1984.

"Rhymes for Old Age" was reprinted in the *Anthology of Magazine Verse and Yearbook of American Poetry*, Monitor Book Company, Inc., Los Angeles, 1985.

"Abandoned House in Late Light," "Blurry Cow," and "Cedar Needles" appeared in *The Morrow Anthology of Younger American Poets*, William Morrow and Company, New York, 1984.

The publication of this book is supported by grants
from the National Endowment for the Arts
in Washington, D.C., a Federal agency,
and the Pennsylvania Council on the Arts.

When the axe came into the forest,
the trees said: the handle is one of us.

—Turkish Proverb

CONTENTS

METEOR SHOWERS, AUGUST, 1968

A night in August,
in my adolescence,
perseveres intact.
An isolated night,
muscular with cold,
pinned open to reveal
a darkened gulf
filled with the talc
of disembodied minerals.

Part of the mind still lies
on a splintery wooden bench,
hostage to the sparks
that brightened
at their moment of extinction.
Austere, remembered acres . . .
embers turning inward
to blueblackness.

Meteors raked the atmosphere,
each one a struck match,
a cat's scratch of light.

Words also fall
across enormous blackness,
small spilled baskets.
Abandoned in that wilderness,
they turn toward one another
and marry, mid-sentence,
becoming in effect
a paradigm of the mind's decorum,
the balance it requires
to hold its illusion of stillness.

It seems that the mind
must renounce
the form that contains it
to swim in the deep,
directionless waters,
or that it must stand
as a stockade or a dam,
opposed to the
starry, immortal flood.

BLURRY COW

Two cows stand transfixed
by a trough of floating leaves,
facing as if into the camera,
black and white. One stamps
at the hot sting of a deerfly.

Seen from the window of a train,
the hoof lifts forever
over hay crosshatched by speed,
and the scales of the haunches
balance. The rest is lost:
the head a sudden slur of light,
the dog loping along the tracks
toward a farm yard
where a woman wavers
in her mirage of laundry.
A blurry cow, of all things,
strays into the mind's eye,
the afterimage
of this day on earth.

IN BED WITH BOOKS

Just before dawn, the dream hung
creaseless as a sheet in heavy dew.
New flowers formed overnight
in the apple tree,
empty as the white arms
of the shirts outstretched
among the branches,
pinned to the damp rope.
My heart was a nest of grass
still restless with old attachments.
I set it high in a froth of blossoms
for the birds to pick clean.

The graph of time
is a faint, arterial blue.
Strung on the orderly latitudes,
no one moment ever touches another,
though they are numerous
as the rising sparks
of a permanent fire.
Summer after summer,
green leaves, wind, gray leaves,
drift in the same nets
as if to sleep, as if love,
like the vagrant perimeters of clouds,
made graphic sense.

Yet I have awakened
in a bed full of books,
free of deep disaffection,
pleased that the sleeping soul
dreams only of the senses.
Such happiness conjugates easily,

unobstructed by the tonnage
of biography, or the unlikelihood
of the heart's revival.
Light in the shape of leaves
plays over the pages tenderly,
as though we knew each other,
and you loved me.

CEDAR NEEDLES

Vendors croon their welcoming harangues
as we pass pyramids of duck eggs,
cheap dresses, black cheeses,
and the shrunken
mummies of the smoked quail,

but we follow the scent of cedar
up into a valley
of sheep and wind-toughened flowers,
the needles
slippery beneath our feet.

Goats scatter uneasily away,
dung rank in their crusted hides.

The rooftops disappear below us,
hazed by the violet smut of cooking.
Here and there the sun
points out a metal gutter.
The clay tiles shiver in the heat.

At this height,
cow bells and church bells
belong to the wild music of the place.
We are farther from God than ever,
at home among the uncountable,
the yellow denial of their split-eyes.

Blighted with plastic flowers,
the homely little cemeteries
embedded in the hillsides
become another landscape
arrested by the camera,

as one tourist
fixes the other there forever.
Strange to think
we have climbed this far
for only another view of ourselves,
the world being
everywhere equally foreign.

THE LATE COMERS

I paid a dollar fifty
for this scrapbook,
these lives asleep in their
patina of dusts and molds.
Despite time's fixatives,
the woman on a bicycle
might have been me,
treading the heavy water
of an uphill ride—
had I been born
in 1910 instead of 1950.

I flip the pages, sparking
the dim detonations
of memory that must be false:
the man and dog
crouch beside a deer,
its head propped on a forked stick.
The baby blurs the moment,
the house drowns in roses.

What if life is nothing
but a series of triggers,
yes/no, right/left, on/off,
like the innards of a calculator?
So that saying a thing one way
eliminates all other ways forever?
That can't be true, can't be true
sing the wheels of the bicycles,
hers and mine,
turning only and always forward,
already late, like us, for something.

PLANET OF SMOKE AND CLOUD

The earth could not keep
its dead in storage.
Cirrus, stratus, the sky
sloughed off their cloudy migrations.
Tides of wars spilled back and forth
across the phantom boundaries
in the naturalization of dust to dust,
dust the pale colors of human countries.
In a brilliancy of particles
the atoms combined and recombined,
flashing in the grim kinetics
of the earth dispersed
back into its elements,
and with everything else:
hydrogen, the rippling fires,
our numberless obsessions
with love and power,
all bathed in the spiritual
phosphorus of the afterglow.
Of all the worlds lost
in the hopeless ascendency
of matter toward God,
one was a fluke of aesthetics.
A hand's rayed bones
could be a bird's wing,
inscrutable fossil
locked in a radiant cinder.

THE MOON IN THE PINES

I do not remember
exactly how the moth
disclosed the blueprint
abridged on its wings,
except that it was August
and the moon fell from a century
unlike the twentieth
into the pines.
This happened on the outskirts
of a town I don't remember.
Starlings drilled for grubs
beneath the deepening neon
of the motel's name
until the moon
cast them back into the shadows.
The air cooled to a resinous perfume,
and a moth made of dark dust
pressed briefly to the screen
a map of unknown regions
now familiar, though
where the heart's grave is,
no one knows.

MY RUBY OF LASTING SADNESS

The Lotus

The ring sparks
in the jeweler's magnifying light.
He tells me the stone
shows stress from every quarter,
I should replace it.
I peer into the leaves
of the lotus enlarged in the glass,
the gold so worn it looks wet,
and see at its center
one live coal spilled from the grate
cracked and flawed
and crossed like a map by many roads.
This is the stone I will keep,
for memory wells
from its red fractures
as though the whole story
were closed up inside it.

Fifteen years ago,
we swam in the icy green
mosaic of the brook,
and lay for a long time
on the warm rocks to dry,
our bodies perfumed
by the pine tar of the soap,
and flecked with lichens.
We were seventeen.

That landscape moulders
deep in ferns and mosses now;
I have visited there in my dreams.

No map shows the whereabouts
of the heart's unchanging homeland
which drifts in the radiant debris
of passing time.
Or locates the house
that hovered in semidarkness
those displaced evenings
when the votive kerosene
longed in its glass column.
The rotting rain barrel
lent the water a taste of earth.
But nothing explains the green heart
that kept on flowering,
always darkening over the years,
until love began its obdurate mutation,
rupturing into the shadowy blossoms
of wood smoke, tarry and fragrant.

One winter night we wandered
deep into the tempered woods,
the sky adrift
in multiple cold petals, cold lights.
From far off we heard
the sensual whack of an axe,
someone splitting the evening's kindling,
and our lungs compressed—
not with joy, but to acknowledge
the durable relic of the moment.

The intervening years
attend at our reunion,
legion of specters thrown
by the restaurant's white candles.

In the bones of his face
I confront the young ghost again,
though a woman knows
when a man has outlived
the love of many women,
as in the way
he opens my hand
and drops into it
his offering:
a ruby in a lotus of gold.

The immature lotus
is prized in Thailand,
where dust presides
over the marriages of children.
The outer leaves are folded back,
exposing the closed blue pod.
He squeezes a lemon
over his artichoke,
and licks astringent juices
from his fingers.
Packed in its tough skins,
the mind arranges its own escape
from such appalling tenderness,
though it lingers
over the marigolds on our table,
their brown areolas,
with the rapt detachment
of a twelve-year-old bride.

I burned the weightless envelopes,
their stamps of monarchs
garish and foreign.

They did not explain anything.
Nothing about the past.
Nothing about grief,
the flame that flares abruptly
up out of the dead coals.
He vanished into a glittering temple,
or stepped into a boat
in the floating market, and was lost.
And though my plighted heart
searched the bazaars of silks and gems,
the embassies, bars, the cheap hotels,
every outlandish, flashy place,
it did not find him.

Fruit picked too soon
never ripens.
Somewhere on earth
he survives unharmed:
blond, half-fledged,
conspicuous in his grace,
unlike this man shrunken
by war, dope, prison, prostitutes,
and casual with guns.
Under immutable skies
he strolls on a beach
stripped white by time, or bathes
in the embalming tides.
He is the green fruit
heavy in the tree
that thrives in the blackened
soil of alien cities,
a ghost, my ghost,
my lotus, my drug, my unripe love.

Bell's Theorem

So we divided the world between us.
He laid claim
to the demimonde,
the fragrant haze of opiates
and dreamy tides of women
whose faces
are the lilies of contentment.
And I retired
to the regions of the north
and made my home
among echoes and shadows.
What is love such that it
opens in the snow
like a crude geranium
and will not stop blooming?
Its atoms do not obey.
It sleepwalks down the hallways
of the empty pines,
tracking the lost
animal of the heart.

What happens is that the heart
becomes itself a refugee,
lugging its suitcase of souvenirs
from place to place.
It is always packing,
leaving for the towns of the past,
which are nowhere on earth.
All obsessions
dress in the clothes
of the one true obsession:
the smoke and tar,

the secret marriage to grief.
The autumn rain
brings down the fleeting pigments,
tears and red leaves.
Love of the world
is love of the ruin.
There is a reference
to something in the self,
a portrait of the face then
in the face now.
Or to the doors
that quietly close to us
that open to others,
so that we turn always
toward the next embrace
hoping that it,
like the first,
will hold us.

And so I kissed some mouths
that did not thrill me,
though they thrilled me
a little later, in retrospect.
Most loves are flurries
in a season unripe for snow.
I could swear that the heart
is miraculous,
a temple of mysteries,
so that faith and endurance
resurrect it whole
and coral-innocent.
It is not so.
If, in its initiation,

it embarks on its one mutation,
the atoms remember.
It is not ever empty again,
but suspends like the bamboo cage
he told me of,
its door ajar
because the bird
was bigger than the hole.
We bear what we are
unable to bear.

In the flux of matter and mechanics,
the bonds of space and time
are unimaginable.
Heaven lowers its ladders
of connective light,
but they are luminous dust
and nothing more.
They sift down
onto the planets,
and onto all the countries
of this planet:
the green ones, gray,
and those in darkness.
Yet somewhere
in the storm of particles
we call this life,
the cache of memory
survives intact.
So we have lived these years
by Bell's Theorem:
that at a fundamental level,
disparate parts of the universe

may make an intimate connection,
and furthermore
that things once joined remain
even over vast distances
and through the shifts of time
attached by an unknown force,
its speed exceeding that of light,
a force which Bell called
"that-which-is."

The physics of connection
is all that matters.
The heart matters, and the mind.
Sensation matters, as long as it lasts.
The world does not think of us at all.
It is animated dust, and that is all,
a flower of atoms pulsing in space,
a flower of ash, a flower of soot.

When snow obliterates the barns
and sighs across the fields,
the porch lights on the farms
glimmer like the last outposts
of human settlement.
I think of things I used to know,
fugitive now in the shadowy
regions of the past,
where the green brook flows.
How like the tremors of cold
they are, leaping suddenly
into the body
as the old connections are made.

A picnic in summer.
The wind rummages
in the leaves of the labrusca,
shaking out the last
flames of the sun.
Drowsy with wine,
my friends and I
follow the barges gliding
on the river far below,
into the fleeting light.
The profound adagio of an axe
carries across the valley.
Then the story stiffens
and comes back to consciousness,
entering the soft
folds of the lotus,
which is always there,
pushing into the whorled red center
as it has a thousand times
over the years,
and repeating this motion,
entering and reentering,
until the heart regains
its sexual ache.
And then I know
I am not where I thought I was,
and that this is the true
nature of the world.
The wind spills through
the leaves of the wild grapes,
and murmurs in the throats
of the empty bottles saying

time breaks everyone's heart
in the end, so drink up.
Its vespers fix this evening too
among the others, the evenings
overlapping like the silver scales
of the river that wells
up out of the hallowed spring
into the unknown.
Far upstream, I will lie down
under the sheltering palms
if my life takes me there,
which it will not,
it is such a small boat, and slow.
But the heart travels
where it will without a passport,
and recognizes no territories.
The ones like me will know me
by these obsequies,
the deepening diffraction in
this red and mortal stone.

JAPANESE WEEPING CHERRY

The bed seems a raft set adrift
in the inadequate moonlight
by which I write.
The weeping cherry
drowns in its blanching waters,
trailing shell-pink sprays
across the screens.

Time is a foreignness
in the forms of things.
Asymmetrical and Japanese,
a tree enters a poem
and is fixed there,
an ignorant stroke of blossoms.
Anything can be corrupted
for the sake of a new pureness.

How easily one form
infects another:
moonlight falters in the leaves,
love holds it there.
The tree becomes
corsages crumbling in a drawer.
And there is never an end to this,
except when consciousness ends,
and it does not end here.

EVENING, HERRON'S FARM

Lit by kerosene,
the windows of the milking barn
recall the dearly departed light.

The basket of early apples
will be heavy by nightfall,
empty again by dawn.

Aligned in the cool apparatus,
the black-and-white bodies shift
and lean, their hooves and udders
shell and ivory
in a realm of little color.
Milk spurts
into the glass globes overhead.

In the old graveyard
the stones have long since
tipped into the lengthening grass.

The animals bide in dusky quarters,
drowsing over the coarse
molasses of fodder.

I can almost penetrate
their remote intelligence,
bedding down in twilight
under the broken music.

Watercress trembles in the brook,
bitter as the wish to come home
to this place,
where all my sufferings
would be imaginable.

A FIRE IN THE MIND

Sputnik, in Russian,
means "traveling companion."
1958: Father lifted his two children
asleep out of the car,
and shook them into sleep's equivalent,
a field of black grasses,
to watch the Soviet spark cross over.

In a photograph, also 1958,
he leans on his long-handled maul,
having split and stacked
what looks like
a snowbank of firewood.
Is that what burns?

Snow slaked his thirst.
He looks as though
he might love
with velocity,
with prowess and strangeness.

My body the orphan
calls out to that parent strangeness.

Not to the love that sleeps in heredity,
but to its counterpart,
the blood stung by companion fire.

Littered with fresh splinters
and the chainsaw's roughage,
the new stump beads with sap.
The green rings tighten in the tree.
After each bisection,
the wind scours
to wound to emptiness.

For love to persist,
the heart must keep its creases
sweet with corroborating dirt.

My father stared up
into the green-black galaxy,
the treasures sunken there.
Even now, years later,
I drift on that worldliness,
all love amassed so far.
I am not a flash of saintly fire.
I slake my thirst where I can,
and rest inside the tiredness
of this the long and only journey,
waking each time
to an advancing sadness and peace.
Each foreign heart
that passes near me
on its unknown trajectory
I call my relative,
my kindling spirit,
another rosy light transporting
its burden of pathos,
its cargo of soil.

OUT OF EARSHOT

A face's final bones
remain inviolate at twenty.

He lifts a half-made fist
to his mouth as if to taste it,
studying himself in the coarse
gray silk of my kimono,
cloth from the sea or from heaven,
scattered with white barnacles.

I can stop in the slender moment
his hand slices the mirror
clean of the shower's steam
and live there a long time.

The simple sleeves become him,
and the length, tied at his hip
with a stone-colored sash.

I could teach him
to be a magnet to the things he loves.

But he is elsewhere, out of earshot,
and does not yet dwell
on the delicacy of hot water,
or the pleasure of the foot
pressed to a grid of cold tiles.

Like the first hard pears of winter,
he will ripen on a snowy afternoon,
within himself a wedding
of the juice to the slight grit.

COLD, SUBSTANTIAL CLOUDS

Stared at long enough,
the sky seems a blackness
into which blue light has fallen,
the faraway flints and micas
of the planets reflecting
each other's glamour infinitely.
A field turned over after harvest
shines like that,
littered with new stones.
And the many surfaces of the sea
flash and fall back
above the unfathomable part,
the ultramarine.

As the leaves come off,
houses appear inside the trees,
houses whose lights in winter
will fix the dark afternoon
to points of whirling snow.
The tall blue doors
of the Catholic church are closed:
gold leaves drift against them.
Inside, the altar
is banked with waxy fires,
though no one kneels or marries,
and no one drifts down the aisle
in robes with a plate of coins.

I could continue,
leaving us out of it,
as though the world spun
in its holy rings without us.
It does not.

Cold, substantial clouds
occlude the planetary blue,
but they are not a boundary.
The great tracts of sky,
divided one from another
by fences of prickling lights,
are all one territory.
Heavenless, we cannot help
but long for other worlds;
they appear in the dilating dark,
flame-colored and perfect.
We cannot keep from ourselves
the desire for perfection,
which is death,
though it is strange to us
as the flammable papers
the birches spill everywhere
around us, which soon become
organic glitter underfoot.

Never mind.
There is comfort in church light,
which is star light incarnate,
and in the miraculous violet
crossed by our shooting lives.

THE HOTEL DU NORD

On the lawn of the old hotel at twilight
a boy stands swathed in a white towel,
his hair still damp from the lake.
The lamps come on
with precocious nostalgia.
Crickets resume in the folds of darkness,
and a boat left empty at the dock
knocks in the negligible waves.
Others have stopped at a spot like this
to listen to a lake's consoling messages.
Through decades of summers
their lowered voices abide,
filtered through the subsequent silences
of love withheld,
or the lies administered
to small ongoing arguments
like fresh bandages, to soothe them.
We stood there too, in northern Wisconsin
in the steadiness of summer,
our children unborn,
our love for one another boundless.
Looking back now
into the vacant twilight of a snapshot,
a reach of fragrant lawn—
the ordinary present darkens
in the tinctures of the past.
But I would not go back to see
the Hotel du Nord loom up again,
its innocent porches, its balconies of hope,
knowing that the paths beside the lake
all lead here, to the one place.
There is no elsewhere.

RELIGIOUS WATER

Staggered by cold and currents,
a man in waders casts
toward a riffle upstream,
teasing the intimate line back in.
The water spills subliminal vowels
around him, and the sound
is an opacity that luck might violate.
His children once were fish
in the passing mystery. And then
a sudden muscle in the old bamboo,
a trout hooked hard in the lip.

A father and a fisherman,
but not at once,
not even in the same thought,
so pure is each.
An ache runs between them
like a fast cold brook.
The netted life
thrashes at that borderline;
the skin of many colors
dries to neutral paper in the creel.
His other wishes swim away
into the icy camouflage,
quick and lost among the dim,
religious voices in the water.

The knife tugs in the belly.
The pearly split, bloodless,
opens on a trove of rosy eggs . . .
which makes the man,
who kneels now on the bank,
shake his head at ignorance.

With only a thumbnail, we can clean away
the tender membrane all along the spine,
and wash into the talking stream
whatever part of human nature
rose toward the iridescence of a cure.

RHYMES FOR OLD AGE

The wind's untiring saxophone
keens at the glass.
The lamp sheds a monochrome
of stainless steel and linens,
the nurse in her snowy dress
firm in her regimens.

The form in the bed
is a soul diminished
to a fledgling, fed
on the tentative balm of spring,
sketch for an angel, half-finished,
shoulder blades the stubs of wings.

Darkened with glaucoma,
the room floats on the retina.
The long vowel of *coma*
broods in the breath, part vapor.
What has become of the penetralia?
Eau de cologne sanctifies the diaper.

Flood and drag, the undertow.
One slips into it undressed,
as into first love, the vertigo
that shrinks to a keepsake of passion.
Sky's amethyst
lies with a sponge in the basin.

WINE

The mint springs up
into lavender mist
after a light rain,
and the lilacs
compound their narcotic perfume.
Outside the kitchen window,
the purple, pointed clusters
spark with droplets, semi-erect.

I no longer wait for anything.
Not for the graphite mutations of evening,
nor for the tranquil fatigue of dawn.
And not for love,
for love dissembles,
escaping each twilight
into the intractable shadow
where the bird music abruptly ceases,
and there is nothing to be done about it.

Guests in the house
do not disturb the pleasing
loneliness of the pears' fragrance,
for no one has followed
the same maps to this moment.
The senses remember what they will.
So that when the soft metals
are stripped from the bottle's neck,
and the residue of soil
wiped away, and the stained cork
drawn out and tenderly sniffed,
no one knows where the others go.

This bottle holds the consonant aromas
of melon and stone,
as though the vines fought drought

and hard ground to open
into this color,
gold grass in another world.
Provoked by the piquant mint,
we each lift a separate glass,
and drink.

When light strikes the frail begonia,
its petals seem to ripen into small fruits.
Now it is evening.
In the cellar, the bottles
continue their disparate evolutions,
each containing a lost afternoon
like today's, the spritz of a rainfall,
or the sediment of a kiss remembered,
gone over and over in the mind,
and still not made permanent.

The yard is fervent with new growth.
Glass in hand,
I walk beneath the lilacs,
green and purple washed
with an undersea nostalgia.
I am always alone.
Spotted and archaic, the tiger lilies
lean in the breezes of the future,
locked in their bunched pods.
We love as many times as we can.
Bouquet is the fugitive
invitation to taste, suggestive
of all there is to be savored.
What I taste in the wine
is my own history,
while all around me
drifts the unconscious scenery.

PAPER WHITE NARCISSUS

Awake or asleep,
the brain dreams at midnight,
roused by the furnace tenderly clanking,
or the errant perfume of the narcissus
forced from midwinter, hard as a kiss.

It dreams its good-bye
to the swindler at the door,
who turns into the granular snow light,
away. And good-bye, tense new hearts
into which the rough hand and its pallor
already have reached.
Grief makes its bouquet the hour
the fire-colored pollen starts to fall.

The wicked flowers of memory
are also white, and bloom anywhere.
Far away, in summer,
the pit loosens in the peach
and the ring slips off
into tall grass, and is lost.
Love comes to nothing.

Nectar dampens the starry clots
that the bees do not visit.
No loveliness, no fragrance or longing
brings on the black honey of forgetfulness
though grief is perennial.

NOT LIKE WATER

Glass dust, crushed cans,
circles of blackened stones:
machine-age glamour
sleeps over the old railroad bed.
No one calls the boxcar home
anymore,
or sweeps the torn-up sidetrack.
A man lived there.
He ate alcohol,
and feared the small boys
under the iron trestle,
their matches and fireworks.
Now, no one.
Lonely o, the whistle
drawn off toward the Rockies,
the rest all consonants.
The grass goes on waving
farewell from the cinders,
miles of sharp-edged greens
troubled in unison
like seaweeds
or the nerves of one mind.
Whatever carries the heart along,
bouyant on emptiness,
black steam,
the waterfall of moments,
is not like water,
is not a river pouring through
its moments all at once,
marrying them, no.

A SUCKLING PIG

What's the difference
between hard and dark?
It stays dark all night.

That's a woman's joke,
prized for the friendly fire it draws,
especially in mixed company.

A joke like that has the ring
of a true story, as does the saying
"a man's brain is in his pants."

The painters and poets all drink
at the Twilight Café,
a farmers' bar on the edge of town,

and that was where Jerome,
the day he sold
the painting of the trailer park,

passed out the invitations
requesting the honor of their presence
among gentlemen of like kind

for an evening of
drunkenness & debauchery,
excesses & excrescences. Black tie.

Jerome proposed to celebrate
three things: his fortieth year,
his rocketing fame, and his divorce.

The women laughed it off.
No one needed to remind us
how high hard drinking counts

among the principles
of thermodynamics.
Art thrives on tension,

yin and yang, their holy friction.
When you live in a small town
in New England,

each shovelful of snow
repeats the credo
or is meaningless exertion.

The month of March
distends with sap and knobby branches.
Tractors rut in the black acres,

the birds come back
to raid the feeders,
cattle emerge from steaming barns.

Jerome ransacked his attic.
The cardboard boxes
crumbled as he opened them:

his grandmother's linens,
limp with age, spilled from tissue,
and through the tarnish

and protective flannels,
silver flashed its costly light.
He had in mind

a feast of visuals:
black, hand-dipped, beeswax
candles from the specialty shop,

red dozens of anthurium,
each waxy, high-veined heart
split by a miniature penis,

curved, pale yellow, dusted with pollens.
Often they had spoken of
the clean dynamic,

how artifice can force
a loveliness from marriages
devoid of loveliness,

as the dented aluminum
and corrugated shadows
of the trailer park

well up in the twilight
Jerome found for them.
They lived entangled

in their brotherhood of work,
where paint and words can spur
anything to tenderness.

At eight o'clock the whole room
rose from a bath of candlelight,
breathing the laden atmosphere

of forced narcissus, so that the air
itself seemed bruisable, and colored
by Scarlatti's luscious harpsichord.

Tucked into each creaseless,
softly folded, immaculate napkin
monogrammed by hand

in another age,
was the crisp, black and gold
foil packet of a condom.

Jerome contrived that his guests
should pass through a doorway into a dream
composed by someone else,

a dream each man could fully enter,
abandoning the old self for a new,
the way a snake bequeaths

its paper ghost to a stone wall.
But at the point where form becomes
determinate, Jerome stopped painting.

The caterers slipped out the back,
leaving behind a suckling pig,
golden, shiny, roasted on its knees,

a wreath of greens around its neck.
Sharpened on a stone, the carving knife
glittered among the smoking candles.

With the sound turned off,
Jerome's expensive video
flickered like the waters of aquariums

at feeding time, nurses and cheerleaders
romping in their luminous elsewhere.
He knew the kind of man

aesthetics could seduce.
Also, they had a history:
the drinking to blackout,

the kidney stones and gout,
and all the vivid, half-believed
versions of their lives before.

So the night was a loaded pistol
right from the start,
a slow burn with a dirt sweetness.

We all make allowances
in the name of humanity,
the name we pray to, if we pray.

But which allowances?
As the first champagne
foamed in the long-stemmed glasses,

Jerome sent his young protégé
down to Springfield to fetch
the entertainment.

Just how detached
should art and artists be?
Did he suspect they'd find

a correlation
in an evening of debauchery?
He must have seen himself

as Bacchus then, plunging with
his flock of satyrs deeper into youth.
Besides, how far is too far?

Once such a question
occurs to a man,
isn't he obliged to answer it?

A man walks into a bar and says,
"Barkeep! Ten shots of your worst scotch."
Pouring the tenth, the barkeep

asks what the occasion is. The man
shudders as the drink goes down.
"Celebrating my first blow-job," he confides.

"No shit," says the barkeep,
reaching for the bottle.
"Here, have one on the house."

"No thanks," says the man.
"If ten shots of that camel piss
won't kill the taste, nothing will."

What's left of the pig
forms their centerpiece,
platter of bones, the head caved in.

For their uniform, they sport
the Mars-black rented tuxedo,
color of the soot that drowns

the candles as the stubs burn down.
Their flags of white linen
are soiled and cast aside.

Fired by brandy, they rise to toast
Saint Jude, patron of lost causes,
who speaks to their stiffening nerve.

The tremulous flames of a birthday cake
appear in the kitchen door,
flanked on either side

by the two muses from Springfield,
crowned by Jerome with plastic ivy.
Cigars flare up like hazard lights.

Large with fraternity,
the white shirts open at the neck,
undone by the slow hypnosis

of women dancing themselves
out of their clothing,
dancing for the faces that form

and reform in the amber smoke,
dancing for men.
A trembling moment comes,

overburdened like liquid in a spoon,
when the boundaries themselves
are the thing that spills.

What begins as a mere flirtation—
the mountain climber starting home
an hour too late,

so that he cannot help but lose
the trail to darkness—
swells to the plural story

of everyone present,
a story of war.
They slip across the lines

in the dark, on their bellies,
tranced by the dream-palette video
pulsing its intimate heat,

its clouds of honey.
The clenched fist and forearm
are a kind of cock.

That moment is followed by another
in which the weapon
no longer seems strange,

and the women's perfume
can be held in the hands
like a bruised peach.

The devil is dissociation.
No one wakes them.
He strings his scabrous wire

around them as they sleep,
stalking in their dreams
the multifarious flesh,

the dresses, damp and confining,
that chafe in the boulevards,
slaves to instinctual fire.

There is another dream
that ends another way.
From high above the curving map,

the explosions resemble floral sea-forms,
huge roses blown open by the storm.
The aircraft trembles in the sweet

air that rises,
green with torn leaves.
Rocking in its harness,

the pilot's camouflage
will slip unnoticed into heaven.
The moment of waking

is a moment of relief.
Gone, the untranslatable troops.
Gone, the trucks that marked

the road with red drippings,
the small, inflaming sun,
the soldier's luck.

The women danced to calm the men.
They danced a dance called
fear of getting caught,

and then the one called
fear of catching something.
They sat in each man's lap

to comfort him, and whispered
private things into his ears,
things with the tongue,

until each longed for the coiled
amnesia of the cobra,
rigid and transfixed

in its straw basket,
caressed by the cold
and hooded music of the flute.

No one expected Jerome's young painter,
newly married, to bolt out the door
with the redhead in tow,

and come downstairs
no more than ten minutes later
for the other one.

The catalog of weapons is endless,
inventions to pry loose
the simple griefs of the world,

and compound them.
Jerome's ex-wife
misunderstood the plan,

and dropped the ten-year-old
off around eleven. Shirttails out,
Jerome carried his son like a baby

into the musical darkness,
the boy's bare feet
latched around his father's waist,

and they danced off-balance
in the guttering candlelight,
the coarse salt of the father's cheek

shielding the child's unblemished face,
the green grass of his breath,
the women laughing and saying

he was handsome like his daddy.
A close call is straw for the fire,
for the smoldering sleep that swallows

even the artillery's close concussions.
All the countries of red clay,
the tricycles and groceries,

were washed away
by monsoons of forgetfulness.
Logy with medals, fictions, old scars,

they bowed their heads
before the holy suckling beast,
which looked like death

if anything ever did,
and drank to it
with glasses uplifted,

those pure pariahs,
to life, to language, and to paint,
and to each other,

because they recognized
the sniper in the soul, and feared
what he might father there that night.

A man calls his wife from the office.
"Honey," he says, "I have some bad news.
You know those stocks I gambled on?

It was a big mistake.
I had to sell the condo in Palm Beach,
the yacht, the string of thoroughbreds,

the ski chalet, and all the cars but two."
"Is that the worst of it?" she wants to know.
"We'll have to let the gardener go,

the butler, and the kitchen staff.
I fear, my love,
you'll have to learn to cook."

"I have a better idea," says the wife.
"Let's fire the chauffeur,
and you can learn to fuck."

WORDS FOR SYNTHESIZER

When I first heard
what a machine could do with music,
I loved the wind a little less.
The trout still rose
through the clean mists
guarding childhood,
making their delicate splash,
but next to the meshing sugars
of a voice fed back to itself,
the splash diminished.

To tell the truth,
I miss the whisper in the mix,
near kiss of mouth and microphone,
and the frictional slide
of fingers on the strings.
They were the first step
toward relinquishment.
But fish-splash and wind
and all loved things
come home to the black sound-box.

The mind's advice to itself
is brainwashing, and it works.
How else could I loll so easily
on the ladder of the years,
the calibrated loneliness
of growing up and old?
It's almost effortless,
now that I find distortion thrilling.

TRANSFIXED BY THE SWIMMERS

Flashy with clean blue chemicals,
the public pool contains the sky
in which the crumpled sheets
of the clouds are soaking.
A man swims his laps there
as if out of habit,
turning his watery face
to the air with each stroke,
as if to me. And just as the
raked red leaves of childhood
ignite in the present
with piercing indiscretion,
so his body streams forward
into the bright rectangle
and back again, a motion
like that of the cold sea
rinsing out its foamy boundaries.

A stony beach extends
as far as summer in another year.
My parents walk
among gelatinous seaweeds
inflated by the sun,
my father with his bathing suit
hitched helplessly in at the waist.
So far out of earshot,
who knows what they say?
Things about money, probably,
the sucking mollusk,
and all their personal dusts and ghosts
tucked into the brainy blue.

The nacreous undersides of clouds
float truthfully overhead.
Infused with pink from above,
they rupture outward,
casting their ragged umbras down.
The careless swimmer
who rises from the water
is no one to me,
though now he will wade
with his white towel up
out of the changeable shadows forever.
The ongoing elastic sky
retains it all.
For after all is dreamed
and written out and of the essence,
the love is not equal to the language.

ABANDONED HOUSE IN LATE LIGHT

A sparrow lights
among the open cones
high in the white pine.
Then slips, a leaf
traveling the green ladders
down to the spiced humus
which feeds on all things
missing, all things lost.
The cloven prints of deer,
a squirrel's immaculate spine,
and somewhere between
the wind and the gray leaves
a far-off waterfall
pours through the cold air,
dismantling a tree,
stripping away the bodies
that the souls may not
linger here among us.
The migrant orioles
disown the paintless birdhouse
vacant in the birch.
Pendulous with grapes, vines
scrawl across the lattice,
scattering raisins
darkened with wine
into the black breakdown of soil.
For years a neighbor swept
the long, cloud-colored
boards of his porch,
and the grit suspended,

like the sound of the axe
in the stacked wood.
Now he lives where even
the wind dissolves,
in a house of breathless passages,
the windows open to birds and snow,
a lock full of rust on the door.

JACK'S FLASHLIGHT

Three years old, my nephew
strafes the dark pines
from the porch with his flashlight.
His father has gone away,
leaving a boat carved from kindling.
Late in August, this far north,
the ground is already cold.
Smoke, pine, and recent rain
will mark this night
and drag it back to him.
I remember when my father
changed the way he loved me.
With my hands over my ears
I watched his power saw
whiten the barn floor
with drifts of sawdust,
sweet burn-smell persisting.
Jack hunches in the chill
intersection of here and now,
and carves at the trees with
the bleaching beam of abandonment.

LET *X*

Let x equal a birthday,
the point at which
the unknown segment of a life
attaches to the known.
Who wouldn't drive a little fast,
dosed with the moon and a red car,
having laughed past midnight
with another woman
about men, how simple they are,
how dangerous,
each one with his own translation,
imagination into love.

I think of the body before
and the body afterward,
its history of counterparts,
the thieves it housed,
the travelers.
A hand on my breast,
where none is now,
a mouth on my mouth,
summoned by the talk of minds
well versed in partial darkness,
the music beating in the radio,
the hazardous moonlit roads.

ELECTRICAL STORM

Beyond the rain
the carbon blue of evening also falls,
the dazzling, distant, wayward blue
of hope, of heaven,
of a lake for drowning.
Unallied to any sadness,
the full-blown lilacs
turn the color of windows,
their roots in scary shadow,
their flowers immortal.
Isn't it prediction
to say the seed
that hardens in a tree
is orphan seed? Or that
branches displaced by wind
are errant bits of destiny?
And does it matter
if it's the ornamental
pruned against doubling
that volunteers itself,
and not the whippet sapling,
the one with a tight life inside it?
Each image elected by the storm
might be the one clearspoken sign:
the leaning barn, the tangled field,
the slur of pale dust in my hand
where the aspirin were.
Ribbons of pallor illuminate
a sky of old newspapers,
unreadable dark print for which
there is no name or paraphrase.

THE ODDS

1.

The maxim "lucky at cards,
unlucky at love" touches
on a truth, but accidentally.
Luck has nothing to do with it.
Luck is a word for ignorance.

Where the river
rushes down to a rocky pool,
boys skinnydip at twilight,
their bodies midsummer brown,
hurling themselves off the high ledge,
plunging into the black,
reflective water.
Driving the back roads
to a poker game,
I've stopped the car
to watch them.
Jackknife, cannonball,
they remind me of twigs
that nearly break
but then unbend
and go on growing,
spring leaves
uncrushing in a muscular,
accelerated splurge
heart-set on summer.
Leaves like my heart,
in which the greensickness
of spring fever lingers.

As I drive on,
the sun sleeps like candlelight
on the barns and sloping fields,

and the rock stars on the radio
come almost close enough to love.
Music, like all sensation
and the passionate mind on paper,
contributes to the fierce
deliciousness of every moment,
and when profound enough
and adamant enough,
engenders hope, an element
one can swim in,
sometimes even drown in.

The idea travels inward,
not outward.
It shrinks and is clarified
in one stroke,
so that it gleams
like a fatal microbe
under the lenses,
a tiny cog, a wheel
spinning with the head-on
inaccuracy of human logic.
Meaning that each card,
depending on its context,
is a source of power
or a source of nothing.

Sometimes the heart
refuses to open,
little wishing-well
choked with pennies.
It knows,
the heart in its heart,
that the odds are against it.

But then the cards can flare
some nights with a force
that must be sexual,
a dark directive
powerful enough
to flow through the deck
and change the outcome,
a sort of voodoo unto oneself.
That's instinct,
experience worked over
until it's second nature,
and with it comes something
that looks like recklessness
but is its opposite.

2.

I thought I knew by heart
every euphemism for expense.
So what new loss unfurls
at the sight of small boys
pushing their bicycles one-handed
along the river bank,
carrying their shoes?
I loved him the way I love
whatever seasons
are not this season.
Loved him for the way
he flinched when I touched him,
suggesting that the first
instant of the future might yield
not just the certainty of pleasure,
but a dose of pain.

In poker,
there's no equivalent for that,
unless it's the innocent
teasing out his final card
in case courtship might help it.
Cards are all clean edges,
and have no memory.

A little awkwardness
equips the soul for love,
and teaches the ear
the faulty music that endures.
The rounded hollow
of the dove's one note,
breath in a bottle,
or wind in water reeds,
played in both
the green wood and the dead.
If God talks to himself
for intimacy's sake,
I've heard him in the papery,
spiritual sound of shuffling.

Would I have thought of it this way
had it been winter, early dark,
snow and taillights
en route to the game?
Would I have pictured
the deck as pure genetics,
the days ahead still crushed
into their earliest forms
like the traits that swim
latent in the blood,
tumor and gift for music alike?

Or listened for the voice
that enters, after the divorce,
a whole new range
inside the old range,
like an injured muscle
learning its new span
as though pain were a fence?
A voice remorseless
in its lust for limits.
But isn't lust
with its formalities
always the driver?
For love and power
and the joyful
transactions of the body?
Not only that.
It rages also,
an appetite for appetites,
disrupting the small
samples of fate
dealt onto the green tablecloth.

3.

I've loved too many times,
and not enough. So what?
I threw the tokens of affection
onto the quieting felt.
They made their own perfection.
The naked boys belong
no more to one world than the other.
They stand for hunger,
which turns the body inward
to feed on itself,

cell cannibalizing cell.
Men love carelessly when young,
women when they're older.
Guilt is a stupid hammer.

Love, money, music, water.
The night blesses them all
equally as it falls,
and does not distinguish between them.
The verb *abandon*
tips on the fulcrum
of its double meaning.

All lives flash and spark,
trailing a lit fuse.
A boy jumps,
and as his small hard body
enters the water,
the ace of hearts
falls onto the green cloth.
I know exactly what it's worth to me
at this moment, which is
the only moment that exists.
The odds are antibodies,
river stones, the leaves
noisy with changing numbers.
Whatever it cost to understand this,
I would pay again.
I pay for my history with my history.
And so I own the rocky pool,
the blue tattoo of love that died,
music from the radio
that is the world.
They are not a part
of what I have agreed to lose.

JOHN JOSEPH IN THE BEYOND (1911–1984)

"I always loved these open fields,
the earth unlocked by rain and plow,
and down along the subtle brook,
a shoal of primulas about to bloom.
And cows, magnificent creatures . . .
they know how to live.

Sitting in the dooryard half asleep,
nearly submerged by snapdragons and herbs,
I ruminated on the silences
that are a form of space.
I sat until my heart
no longer frightened me.

Now I travel with the wind
through leaves and flowers,
our two voices interlaced.
What I so often called the infinite,
eternal—half in jest, of course
(irony and hunger being

the only true laws of nature)—
I can no longer apprehend.
The tenses flex as one muscle,
and I laugh at the times
I held the seasons separate in my mind
as if they were not one fruit, one ocean.

Oh, I am laughing, never fear,
with Leopardi and my dear Augustine,
asking my favorite question once again,
deepened now by hindsight's piquant spark:
if the past and the future exist,
where are they?"

THE COLORLESS CENTER OF EVERYTHING

At the center of the wet clay
lithe in the potter's hands
is the shape of the new bowl, invisible.
A cross-section of the full spectrum
shows the same colorless zero
at the core, the point at which
all colors neutralize and vanish,
darken to extinction. All except violet,
the unreasonable color, the color of sex.
Thus we converse not in the
psychologically primary hues,
but in terra cotta, Egyptian green,
burnt sienna, cerise. . . .

Peruvian lilies in a clay bowl
consist of primary pigments and light.
Inside each yellow flower stitched with red
the iridescent pollens cling,
alien dust the traveler brings
home with the long green stems.
The bowl is glazed blue-black.

Inside the woman's body
is the colorless center of marriage,
against which the man hardens himself.
The bowl of flowers is simply
his gift to her.
The third part is their subtext,
an emptiness complete in itself
like the space between them as they sleep,
or the night sky,
blue-black and monochromatic.
So that our lives resemble
the truculent harmonies in the prism,
but with black mixed in.

TRANSLATIONS FROM THE RATIONAL

The roofless houses by the roadside drown
in sky the color of mercurochrome.
Greener than snow, the acres of limestone
force new beauty from a simple noun,
the last of the five elements: bone.
Without a place to rest, the remnant sounds
of aftermath pray to the empty towns
for resurrection of the chromosome.
The distant roses of plutonium
make of the sky a staggering bouquet
turned in upon itself, a cranium
packed with scenes from life, a matinée
of dreams for the millennium,
the lit terrain we called the Milky Way.

Across the bulging, dust-dark summer storm,
lightning prints a jagged, branching track.
Nostalgia's not a longing to go back,
nor love of the world a love of form.
Not quite. We glimpse another paradise
obscured by its protective colorations,
but lose it to a flux of short durations.
All that we love, we try to memorize.
Time undermines that love. Each tense collides,
a broken storm of many blossomings.
The nets we throw out drag the wayward tides
for things lost long ago to the water's rings.
we watch the speckled, paling undersides
of those quick fish, the vanishing evenings.

ASLEEP IN THE HEAT

Whatever flowers were about to bloom
are blooming now, their fragrance
arriving on currents of air
that scarcely move,
a blanket over me, a weight
like that of the dream I dream
to illustrate the sexual world,
its many invitations.
I dream that an orange ray
falls on the bookcase, a light
disturbing in its beauty
since I am alone,
and I reach for the camera downstairs
though it is useless
to try to hold such a goldenness still.
I stay asleep, crossed twice
by white skin the sun was denied,
and the heat feels as water does
to a good swimmer: affectionate.

PARTITA FOR SOLO VIOLIN

What comes to mind is a pond
clotted with lilies, a black pond,
though the blackness may be
nothing more than afterthought
overlaid on the green water.
Lilacs break along the shore,
damp white clusters
throwing back starlight
and the smell of sleep.
In what world do I wake?

Snows sweep in to tranquilize
places disturbed by holiness.
The lilies withdraw,
and the ice forms a thick lens
through which I see
the candles of lost love
glimmering still.
But stars make a light
like that in the cold crystals
regardless of histories.

A hound mourns in the pine
undercurrents of the wind.
Lilies in cellophane.
The smell of the cut-off stems.
A host of whittling flames
illuminates the private shrines
and spills a cuneiform
queer as bird tracks on the snow.
A score for human voice,
a score for strings.

The charring sky lets fall
the first notes, showers of embers
spawned in the final black.
I forage in that night for them,
tracking the cool vestiges
far into silence.
Like the wasps I have built
a tenement of paper,
hole upon hole of storage,
the imaginer's emblem and home.

Surrounding currents bear away
this crude notation. It rides
on water dark with history,
not starlessness. I conceive of
a music crushed from earthly loves,
each note contributing
its lilacs, its snowbanks, its dead
dragged in the undertow. A music
composed of vital sparks, but played
with a plaintive and funeral coloring.

For Ann Martin Chase & Charles Pratt Twichell

In the tension of opposites, all things have their being.

—Heraclitus

PITT POETRY SERIES

Ed Ochester, General Editor

Dannie Abse, *Collected Poems*
Claribel Alegría, *Flowers from the Volcano*
Jon Anderson, *Death and Friends*
Jon Anderson, *In Sepia*
Jon Anderson, *Looking for Jonathan*
John Balaban, *After Our War*
Michael Benedikt, *The Badminton at Great Barrington; Or, Gustave Mahler & the Chattanooga Choo-Choo*
Michael Burkard, *Ruby for Grief*
Kathy Callaway, *Heart of the Garfish*
Siv Cedering, *Letters from the Floating World*
Lorna Dee Cervantes, *Emplumada*
Robert Coles, *A Festering Sweetness: Poems of American People*
Leo Connellan, *First Selected Poems*
Kate Daniels, *The White Wave*
Norman Dubie, *Alehouse Sonnets*
Stuart Dybek, *Brass Knuckles*
Odysseus Elytis, *The Axion Esti*
John Engels, *Blood Mountain*
Brendan Galvin, *The Minutes No One Owns*
Brendan Galvin, *No Time for Good Reasons*
Gary Gildner, *Blue Like the Heavens: New & Selected Poems*
Gary Gildner, *Digging for Indians*
Gary Gildner, *First Practice*
Gary Gildner, *Nails*
Gary Gildner, *The Runner*
Bruce Guernsey, *January Thaw*
Mark Halperin, *Backroads*
Michael S. Harper, *Song: I Want a Witness*
John Hart, *The Climbers*
Gwen Head, *Special Effects*
Gwen Head, *The Ten Thousandth Night*
Barbara Helfgott Hyett, *In Evidence: Poems of the Liberation of Nazi Concentration Camps*
Milne Holton and Graham W. Reid, eds., *Reading the Ashes: An Anthology of the Poetry of Modern Macedonia*
Milne Holton and Paul Vangelisti, eds., *The New Polish Poetry: A Bilingual Collection*
David Huddle, *Paper Boy*
Lawrence Joseph, *Shouting at No One*

Shirley Kaufman, *From One Life to Another*
Shirley Kaufman, *Gold Country*
Ted Kooser, *One World at a Time*
Ted Kooser, *Sure Signs: New and Selected Poems*
Larry Levis, *Winter Stars*
Larry Levis, *Wrecking Crew*
Robert Louthan, *Living in Code*
Tom Lowenstein, tr., *Eskimo Poems from Canada and Greenland*
Archibald MacLeish, *The Great American Fourth of July Parade*
Peter Meinke, *Trying to Surprise God*
Judith Minty, *In the Presence of Mothers*
Carol Muske, *Camouflage*
Carol Muske, *Wyndmere*
Leonard Nathan, *Carrying On: New & Selected Poems*
Leonard Nathan, *Dear Blood*
Leonard Nathan, *Holding Patterns*
Kathleen Norris, *The Middle of the World*
Sharon Olds, *Satan Says*
Greg Pape, *Black Branches*
Greg Pape, *Border Crossings*
James Reiss, *Express*
Ed Roberson, *Etai-Eken*
William Pitt Root, *Faultdancing*
Liz Rosenberg, *The Fire Music*
Eugene Ruggles, *The Lifeguard in the Snow*
Dennis Scott, *Uncle Time*
Herbert Scott, *Groceries*
Richard Shelton, *Of All the Dirty Words*
Richard Shelton, *Selected Poems, 1969-1981*
Richard Shelton, *You Can't Have Everything*
Arthur Smith, *Elegy on Independence Day*
Gary Soto, *Black Hair*
Gary Soto, *The Elements of San Joaquin*
Gary Soto, *The Tale of Sunlight*
Gary Soto, *Where Sparrows Work Hard*
Tomas Tranströmer, *Windows & Stones: Selected Poems*
Chase Twichell, *Northern Spy*
Chase Twichell, *The Odds*
Constance Urdang, *The Lone Woman and Others*
Constance Urdang, *Only the World*
Ronald Wallace, *Tunes for Bears to Dance To*
Cary Waterman, *The Salamander Migration and Other Poems*
Bruce Weigl, *A Romance*
David P. Young, *The Names of a Hare in English*
Paul Zimmer, *Family Reunion: Selected and New Poems*